# Gran. to Stay

Written by Jill Eggleton
Illustrated by Kelvin Hawley

"I have come
to stay,"
said Granny.

"I have bags

and boxes."

"I have
my plants,"

said Granny.

"I have my fish.

I have my birds.

And I have
my mice."

The kids put the

bags  and

the boxes

in the house.

## "Wow!"
said the kids.

"We can not see
the window."

The kids put

the plants  in

the house. They put

the fish and

the birds and

the mice

in the house!

9

**"Wow!"**
said the kids.

"We can not see
the bed!"

Where can
Granny stay?

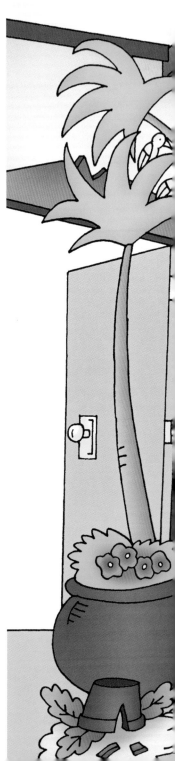

"Here," said Granny.

"Come and
look at me.
This is where
I will stay."

# "Wow!"

said the kids.
"We will stay here, too!"

# Labels

# Guide Notes

**Title: Granny Comes to Stay**

**Stage:** Early (2) – Yellow

**Genre:** Fiction

**Approach:** Guided Reading

**Processes:** Thinking Critically, Exploring Language, Processing Information

**Written and Visual Focus:** Labels

**Word Count:** 110

## THINKING CRITICALLY

(sample questions)

- What do you think this story could be about?
- Focus on the title and discuss.
- Discuss what is unusual in the cover picture.
- Why do you think Granny brought so many things when she came to stay?
- What do you think Granny could have had in all the boxes and bags?
- What else do you think the kids could have done with the boxes and bags?
- Why do you think the kids wanted to sleep in the tent?

## EXPLORING LANGUAGE

### Terminology

Title, cover, illustrations, author, illustrator

### Vocabulary

**Interest words:** bags, boxes, plants, birds, mice, tent, wow

**High-frequency words (reinforced):** come, to, I, have, said, and, my, the, put, in, can, not, they, we, here, look, at, me, this, is, will, too

**New words:** stay, see, where

**Positional word:** in

### Print Conventions

Capital letter for sentence beginnings and names (**G**ranny), full stops, quotation marks, commas, question marks, exclamation marks